Marian McPartland
Willow Creek
and other ballads

Contents

Marian McPartland has many albums, cassettes and Compact Discs on the Concord label. For a complete list, please send for a free catalog to CONCORD RECORDS, P.O. Box 845, Concord, CA 94522.

Music Editors: Bill Galliford & David Pugh
Production: David C. Olsen
Album Cover Art: © 1985 Concord Jazz, Inc.
Used by Permission
Illustration: Tom Burgess

Transcriptions by Ellen Rowe

2

Marian McPartland

In her long career as a working jazz musician, Marian McPartland has in the estimation of *The New Yorker* critic Whitney Balliet, "moved beyond adroit adulation into her own special realm. It is, in the way of Johnny Hodges and Sidney Bechet and Tatum, an emotional, romantic and highly inventive one." The McPartland style is flexible and complex, and almost impossible to pigeonhole. Audiences who type her as a modern player, light-fingered and elegant, may be surprised by a rollicking left-handed romp through the blues. Listeners looking for an orthodox diet of American Popular Songs will find their Berlin, Arlen and Kern punctuated occasionally with Lennon and McCartney. Marian ranges happily across the landscape of jazz, from Hoagy Carmichael to Chick Corea. She plays Dixieland and bebop with aplomb, and seems equally comfortable improvising on the theme from Sesame Street and trading staccato runs with McCoy Tyner. She'll play almost anything, but her touch and talent are most impressive on ballads. The form suits her. She is the best sort of musical conservative, demonstrating her respect for the traditions of the past by bringing them exuberantly up to date. Listening to Marian McPartland play, you can almost hear the music evolve. "She is an exceptionally lyrical ballad performer," Leonard Feather writes, "enriching and expanding the harmonic and melodic essence of every theme."

Now she tackles Stevie Wonder's *"All in Love is Fair,"* a lovely progression of simple minor chords. On her first few attempts she ornaments extensively, embroidering, adding texture to the tune. Then she reverses direction and begins to pare the piece down, eliminating any excess, cutting and trimming until she's sculpted something extraordinarily fine. She locates a haunting undertone beneath the song's surface, like smoke in a fog, and refines it with each successive take. The melody is built around a few linked phrases, but she invests them with emotional resonance and makes them seem like much, much more.

It is characteristic of Marian's approach that she simplifies where someone else might complicate. "I've been trying to play *less*," she says. She makes Dave Brubeck's *"Summer Song"* a wistful daydream, as if wading in the warm shallows of a lake, and captures its soul that way. She roasts and old chestnut *("I've Got A Crush on You")* in an entirely new manner, adding a dash of dignity and bearing. Then, as a personal and deeply moving elegy, offers *"Blood Count"* in startling contrast. "Stan Getz plays that tune," she says, "and hearing his version is what made me want to learn it. I don't know, though. It kind of scares me. I'm afraid it'll make people throw themselves out windows." She understands intuitively that ballads, like the blues, can span a full spectrum of emotional colors.

Marian hates wasting time, and it isn't long before she completes a solid album's worth of material, but she seems reluctant to let go. Alone with a perfectly tuned piano, she has conjured a whole world, and she'd like to linger there a few minutes longer in hopes of discovering something more. It is this trait most of all that distinguishes her playing. Marian McPartland never stops exploring. She's kept her curiosity, her love of a musical mystery, her pure sense of pleasure as she plays. At a time when other artists might be inclined to slack off, she works harder than ever, mapping the intimate territory of "her own special realm." "I try not to play the same tunes all the time," she told me once, "and when I do, I try to play them a little differently. I try to keep learning. I think I'm getting better — at least some of the time. Of course, there are times when you play terribly, but I really do feel as if I'm improving." She smiled. "I think my best virtue is persistence," she said. "I'm still doing my own thing."

J. Tevere MacFadyen
(J. Tevere MacFadyen writes about
jazz for several national publications.)

WITHOUT YOU

By AHMAD JAMAL

G7(♭9 ♯11 ♭13)
C7(♭5 ♭9)
Fmaj9
Em11
G/A
Dmaj9
Più mosso
G
G♯m11
G♯m7
mf
F♯m7
B13
B7
Em7
A13
A7
A♭m7(4)
A♭m7/D♭
Am7(4)/D
Am7/D
G
G♯m11
G♯m7
F♯m7
B13
B7
Em7
A13
A7
E♭m7/A♭
8va
N.C.

6

Em7
A13
A7
A♭m7(4)
A♭m7/D♭
Am7(4)/D
Am7/D
G
G♯m11
G♯m7
F♯m7
B13
B7
Em7
A13
A7
E♭m7/A♭
N.C.
8va
Tempo I
C/A♭
loco
rit.
D♭/A
D/B♭
E♭/B
cresc.
E/C
F/D♭
rit.
G♭/D
G/E♭
A♭/E
A/F
cresc.
8va
loco

8

WILLOW CREEK

By MARIAN McPARTLAND
and LOONIS McGLOHON

C(2)
D(2)
D
A/D
D6
C
Tempo ♩= 84
B♭maj7/C
Fmaj9
Fm9
A♭maj7/B♭
E♭maj9
B♭
A♭/B♭
G♭/B♭
B♭7(♭5 ♭9 ♭13)
E♭maj13
E♭maj9
Am7/D
D
D7(♯5 ♯9)
D7(♭5 ♭9)
D7(♯5 ♯9)
D7(♭5 ♭9)
G(2)
F(2)

Dmaj6/9
Cmaj6/9
D
E/D
F♯/D
D
C(2)
Gm7/C
B♭maj7/C
Fmaj9
Fmaj6/9
A♭maj7/B♭
B♭
A♭maj7/B♭
E♭maj13
B♭
A♭/B♭
Gm/B♭
B♭7(♭5 ♭9)
E♭maj9
Am7/D
Gm9
C13
Fmaj6/9
C13
G♭13
cresc.
mf

Fm9
B♭13
E♭maj13
E♭maj9
E♭m9
A♭13
cresc.
D♭maj13
f
D♭6
D♭maj9
B♭(2)
E♭maj9(♯11)
A7(♭9 ♭13)
A♭7(♯11)
dim.
G
mf
Fmaj6/9
D(2)
Cmaj6/9
D
D
E/D
D
C
Cmaj9

C/D Bm/D Am/(D) (D13) C/(D) G♯dim7/(D) Am7/(D) (D13♯11) Bm7
Em11
Bm
Am7(4)
A♭13(♯11)
G♭13(♯11)
A♭13(♯11)
G♭13(♯11)
rit.
A♭13(♯11)
rit.

THE THINGS WE DID LAST SUMMER

Words by SAMMY CAHN
Music by JULE STYNE

Bm7(♭5) B9(♭5) E7(♭9 ♭13) Am9 Cm(maj7) Bm7 Em7
mf
dim.
mp
Am7(4) Am7/D D9 Bm7(4) E13 Am7 D13 G G♯dim7
rit.
accel.
Am9 Am/D D7(♭9) Gmaj9 F♯6/G G6 F♯6/G Gmaj13 Bm7(♭5) B9(♭5) E7(♭9 ♭13) E7
cresc.
mf
rit.
Am Cm(maj7) Bm Em7 Em9 Em7 Am7(4) Bm7 Cmaj7 C/D
dim.
Gmaj13 Dm7/G G7 Dm7/G G13 (D♭7)
mp
3
3

Cmaj9
G7(♭13)
Cmaj9
Dm7
Em7
Em(2)
Em
Gmaj7/A
A7
Em7/A
A13
D
C♯dim7/D
Am7/D
D7(♭9)
G
G♯dim7
Am9
Am/D
D13(♭9 ♯11)
cresc.
Gmaj9
Gmaj6/9
F♯6/G
Gmaj6/9
F♯6/G
G(2)
mf
Dm/F
E7(♭9)
Am7
Cm(maj7)
Bm7
Em7
Am7(4)
D9
G/D
B♭/D
D7(♭9)
G/D

A♭/D
D7
G
G♯dim7
Am7
Am7/D
D7(♭9)
G
Gmaj9
Bm7(♭5)
E7sus
E7(♭9)
Am7
F13(♯11)
Bm7
Em7
E7
Am7
D9
Bm7
B7
Em7
B♭9(♯11)
A13
A♭7
G(2)
E7(♭9)
Am11
Am7
Am/D
D7(♭9)
Gmaj9

18

Faster
Am7/D D7(♭9) G G♯dim7 Am9 Am7/D D7(♭9)
dim. rit. mp cresc. rit.
Gmaj9 G6 Gmaj9 G6 F♯/G G(2) Bm7(♭5) B7(♭5) E7(♭5 ♭9 ♭13) Am9 Cm(maj7)
mf accel. rit.
Bm7 Em7 Am9 Am7/D D7 Bm7(♭5) E7(♭9 ♭13) Am7
rit.
Cm9 F7(♯11) Gm7 Am7 B♭m7 Bm7 C♯dim G/D F13 F9 E7(♭13) E7(♭5 ♭9)
rit. rit.
A(2)/G
B/A Am7 C/D D13(♭9) E♭maj9 A♭maj9(♯11) G♭maj9 Amaj9 G(2)
dim. mp

ALL IN LOVE IS FAIR

By STEVIE WONDER

All in Love Is Fair - 5 - 1

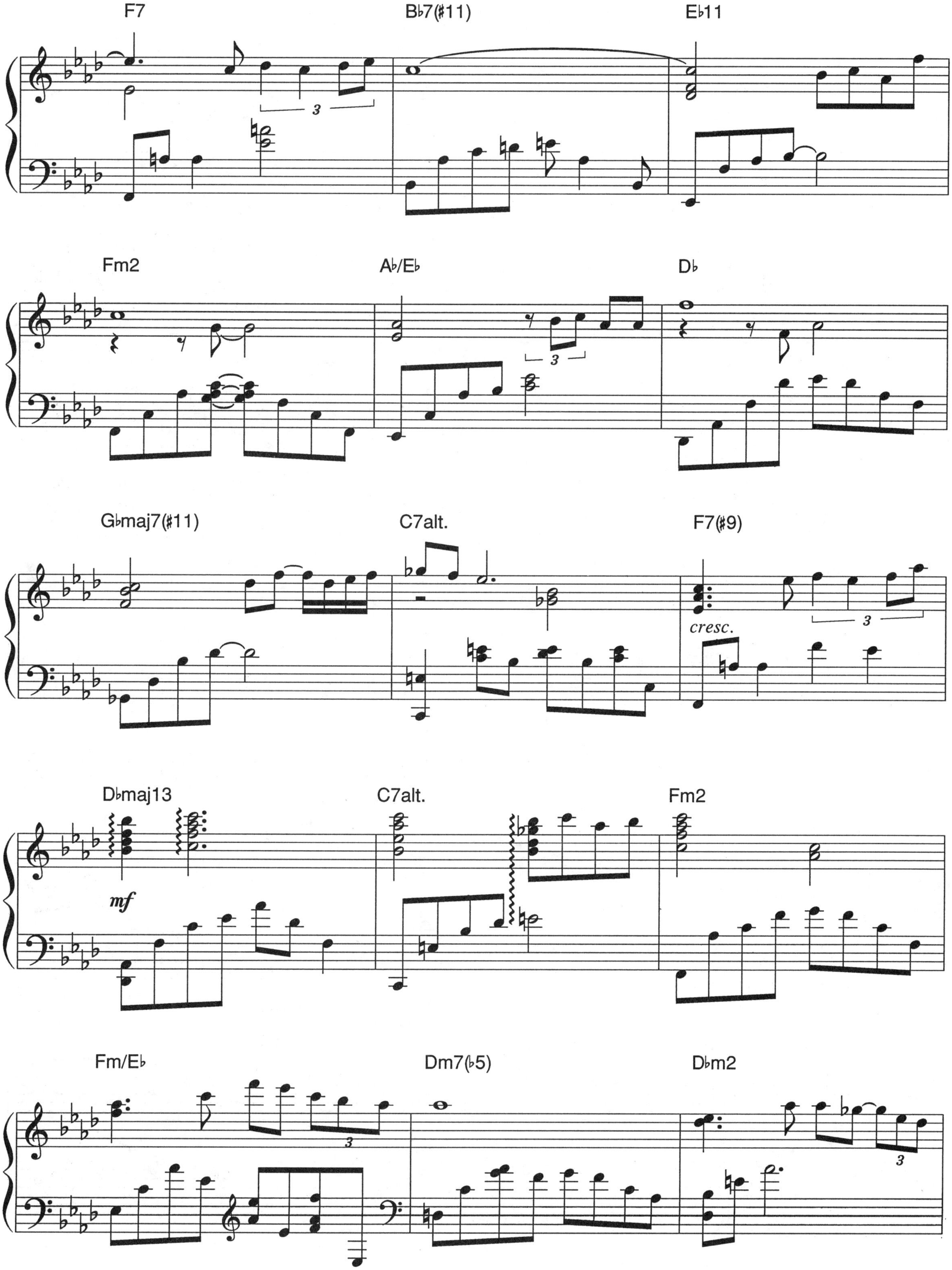
F7
B♭7(♯11)
E♭11
Fm2
A♭/E♭
D♭
G♭maj7(♯11)
C7alt.
F7(♯9)
cresc.
D♭maj13
mf
C7alt.
Fm2
Fm/E♭
Dm7(♭5)
D♭m2

Cm7
A♭2/C
F7(♯9)
F7(♭9)
B♭m9
E♭11
A♭6
C7(♭9)
Fm
Fm(♯7)
Cm7/E♭
Dm7(♭5)
D♭
D♭maj7
G♭maj7
C7alt.
F7
B9
B♭13
E♭11
Fm11
A♭maj7/E♭
D7(♭9 ♯5)
D♭maj9
G♭maj7(♯11)

C7alt.
F7(♭5)
D♭maj13
C7alt.
Fm2
A♭maj7/E♭
Dm7(♭5)
D♭m
A♭2/C
F7(♭9 ♯5)
B♭m9
E♭11
Fm7
G♭maj7
Fm
Fm7/E♭

24

BLOOD COUNT

By BILLY STRAYHORN

Gm13
C13
Fmaj9
E13
A13
B♭13
B13
C13
Tempo I
F9(♯11)
dim. e rit.
mp
B♭7(♯5)
E9(♭5)
E♭9(♯11)
A9(♭5)
D
3
D+
D
D9sus
Dm7
D7(♭9)
gradually into tempo
= 68-72
G6/9
C9
A
A/D
Bm7
3

E13
B♭13(♯11)
D2/A
F2/A
6
G9/A
A13
Dmaj13
F9(♯11)
B♭7(♯5)
E9(♭5)
E♭9(♯11)
A9(♭5)
Dm
B♭/D
Dm
D9sus
D7(♯9)
F9(♯11)
B♭7(♯5)
E9(♭5)

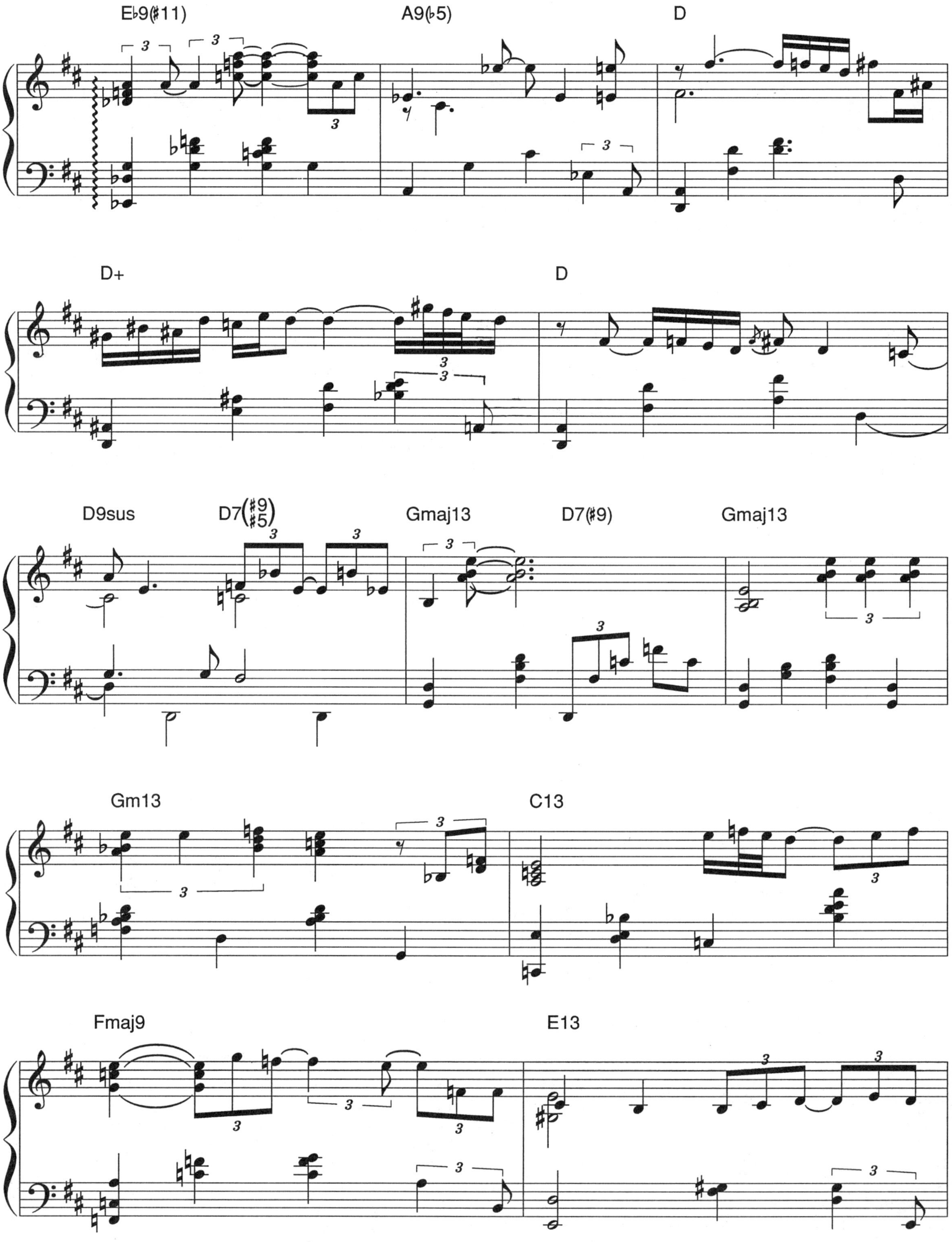
E♭9(♯11)
A9(♭5)
D
D+
D
D9sus
D7(♯9/♯5)
Gmaj13
D7(♯9)
Gmaj13
Gm13
C13
Fmaj9
E13

Freely
A13
B♭13
B13
C13
F9(♯11)
B♭7(♯5)
E9(♭5)
E 9(♯11)
A9(♭5)
D
D+
D
D9sus
A♭7
Gmaj7
C13
Dmaj9/A
B♭dim
Bm9
E13(♭9)
B♭13
D2/A
Fmaj7/A
A11
A7(♯9 ♭5)
Dm7
E/D
E♭/D
D
D2
molto rit.
pp

LONG AGO AND FAR AWAY

Words by IRA GERSHWIN
Music by JEROME KERN

Long Ago and Far Away - 4 - 1

Bbm7 Eb13 Abmaj6/9 Gdim7 Fm Adim7/F# Bbm9 Eb7 Cb Ab
Dbm7 Gb13 Cbmaj9 Abm9 Fm11 Fm7/Bb Ebmaj6/9
Dbmaj7/Eb Cm7 F7(b9 #9)/A Bbm9 Eb13 A7(b5)
cresc.
Ab6 Fm7 Bbm11 Eb13/Db Cm7 Fm9
f
Cm/Bb Bbm7 Eb9 Cm7(4) Fm7 Bbm7 Eb13(#11) Eb7

A♭6
Gdim7
Fm7
Adim7/F♯
B♭m11
E♭7
E♭m9
E♭m9/A♭
3
3
A♭13(♭9)
D♭maj7
3
3
G♭9
A♭(2)/E♭
A♭dim/E♭
B♭m7/E♭
E♭13(♭9)
dim.
E(2)
Amaj7
Gmaj7
Fmaj7
D♭maj7
Amaj13
B/A
mf
rit.
A♭
Fm
B♭m7
E♭13
Cm
Fm9
3
3

Bbm13 Bbm7 Fm/Eb Eb7 Ab6/C Fm Bbm7 Eb13(#11)
3
3
Abmaj6/9 C7 Fm F13(b9) Bbm9 Eb9 Ebm11 Ebm7/Ab A13 Ab13
cresc.
3
f
cresc.
Db Dbmaj7 Gb13 Gb13(#11) Gb13 Ab(2)/Eb Abdim Db/Eb Eb13
ff
dim.
f
dim.
C7alt Fm9 Bbm7 Eb13 Emaj7 A Fmaj7 Dbmaj7
mf
dim.
3
mp
Abmaj7 Emaj7 Dmaj9 Eb7(#9) Ab(2)
8va
8va

I'VE GOT A CRUSH ON YOU

Words by IRA GERSHWIN
Music by GEORGE GERSHWIN

Strum strings inside piano

(with pedal)

Ballad ♩= 69
D13 G9sus Cmaj7 Em E♭dim7 Dm7 G13
Cmaj7 Em E♭dim7 Dm7 G9 Cmaj7 Am9
D9sus D9 D9sus D7 G7sus D7(♭9) G11 G7(♭9)
Cmaj7 Em E♭dim7 Dm7 G13 Cmaj7 Em7 E♭dim7
Dm9 Bm7(♭5) E7(♭9 ♯5) Am11 Am/G F♯m7(♭5) G/F F G/F F

Em11
Am9
Dm9
G11
Emaj9/C
A♭/G
Cmaj9/G
Dm11
D♭maj7(♯11)
C
Em7
E♭dim7
Dm9
D♭7
C2
Em7
E♭dim7
Dm7
G9sus
G7
C2
Am7
D9
D9sus

D9 D7(♯9) D7sus D♭7
C Em7 E♭dim7 Dm7 G13
Freely
C Em7 E♭m7 Dm9 Bm7(♭5)/E Am11 Am9/G
F♯m7(♭5) F7 B7 Cmaj7 Em7 Am11 C6 Dm9 G11 E7(♯9) A9sus A7(♭9)
Dm9 Em7 Fmaj7 G9sus G7 C F/C C G/F F E7(♯9) A2
Strum strings inside piano
mp

SUMMER SONG

By DAVE BRUBECK

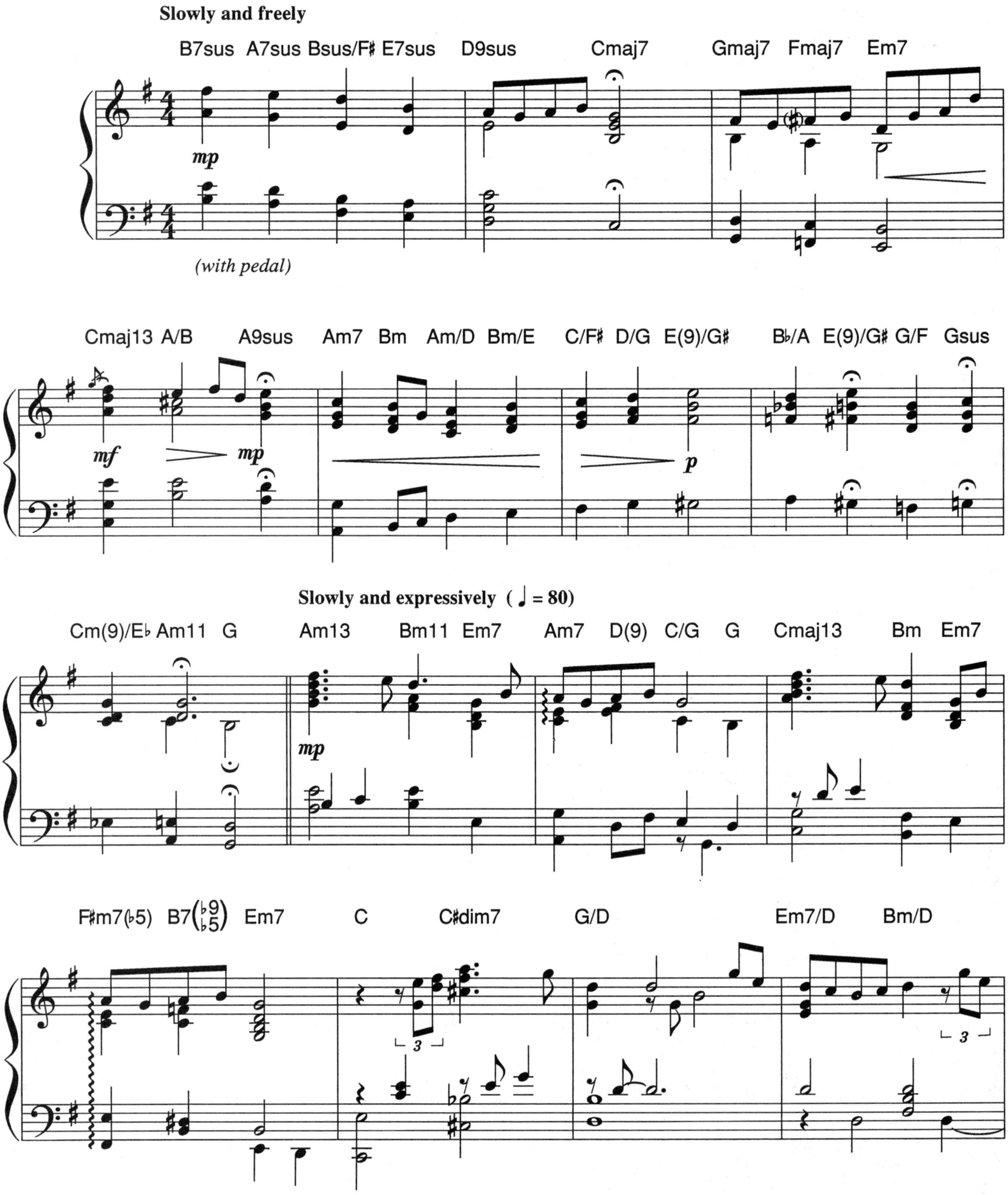

D9sus Bm11/F♯ Em7 Cmaj13 Bm7 Em7 Am7 D9sus C/G G Cmaj13 Bm7
a tempo
rit.
p
mp
F♯m7(♭5) B7(♭9/♭5) Em7 C C♯dim7 G(9)/D
3
D9sus G(9)/D C Bm7 Em9 G(9) Em
Faster
poco rit.
L.H.
A/C♯ D7/C G/B C/E D9 Gmaj7 Em7 Asus A7 D/A
mf
D G/B Am G♯dim7 Am7 D7 Gmaj7 Am7 Bm7 Em A13 G/B A9
dim. e rit.

Meno mosso
C7(♯11) Bm7 Em7 Am7 D9sus C/G G C7(♯11) Bm7 Em7
mp
F♯7(♯9) B7(♭5) Em7 Gmaj7/D Cmaj7 C♯dim7 G/D C/D
3
mf
poco a accel.
3
L.H.
Bm/D Am/C G6/9 C Bm7 Em2
3
L.H.
dim.
mp
poco rit.
Freely and expressively
Gmaj7 Em11 Gmaj7/D A13 D9sus Bm7 Em7 Am7 D7 Bm/E Em11
mf
A9sus A13 D(9) D7 G F♯m7(♭5) G7/F C/E Cm6/E♭
3

G/D Am/C Bm Em7 A13 G9/B A7/C♯ F♯7(♯5) F♯7(♯9) Bm7 Em7
6
f
A13 Dm9 D13(♭9) C/G G Cmaj13 Bm7 Em7 F♯m7(♭5) B7(♭9 ♭5) B7(♭9)
dim.
poco rit.
Em7 Cmaj9 C♯dim7 G/D C/G
mf
mp
Bm Am G Am Bm Cmaj9 Bm E
p
mp
molto rit.
p
8va

Ellen Rowe

Ellen Rowe is currently Director of Jazz Studies at the University of Connecticut, teaching Jazz Piano, Jazz Arranging, Jazz Improvisation and directing the University of Connecticut Jazz Ensemble. She is a graduate of the Eastman School of Music where she received the Bachelor of Music degree and the Masters degree in jazz composition and arranging. In 1982 she received the Best Original Composition Award in the *Downbeat* Magazine Student Recording Awards Contest.

Ms. Rowe has had compositions and arrangements performed by the Mel Lewis Orchestra, London Symphony Orchestra, Concordia, NY Pro Arte Chamber Players, Rochester Philharmonic and other major orchestras, and is currently arranger/transcriber for Marian McPartland.

Ms. Rowe has performed as a jazz pianist throughout Europe and Scandinavia and recently was guest soloist with the Little Orchestra of New York in a performance of "Rhapsody In Blue" at Avery Fisher Hall. In April of 1990 she was a guest on "Marian McPartland's Piano Jazz" on National Public Radio.

In addition to her freelance work as a composer and pianist, Ms. Rowe is active as a clinician, adjudicator and guest artist at schools throughout New England and was selected as the conductor for the 1989 Connecticut All-State Jazz Ensemble and 1990 Massachusetts All-State Jazz Ensemble.